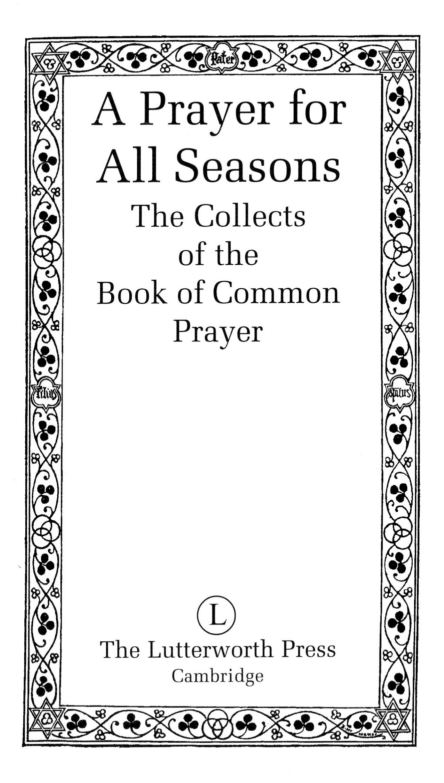

# A Prayer for All Seasons

## The Collects of the Book of Common Prayer

The Lutterworth Press

Cambridge

The Lutterworth Press
P. O. Box 60
Cambridge
CB1 2NT

e mail: publishing@lutterworth.com
web site: http://www.lutterworth.com

British Library Cataloguing in Publication Data:
A catalogue record is available from the British Library

ISBN 0 7188 2994 8 paperback
ISBN 0 7188 2995 6 cased

Printed by
The Cromwell Press Ltd, Trowbridge

# ACKNOWLEDGEMENTS

The illustrations are based on wood engravings designed by
Blanche McManus for *The Altar Service Book* edited by Vernon
Staley (1903).

Extracts from *The Book of Common Prayer* (1662) are
reproduced by permission of Cambridge University Press.

An earlier version of *A Prayer for All Seasons*, compiled by
Vivien Morris, was published by Fort House in 1987.

# CONTENTS

The Book of Common Prayer has been the spiritual resource of English and English speaking people for four centuries. It is a book of prayer for the whole community, devised and composed so that it might satisfy everyone. Cranmer looked to the past as well as the present when he set about this task at a time of reformation and change. The language he employed was quite deliberately "not of an age, but for all time".

The language of Cranmer's Prayer Book has survived because it has shown itself sensitive to the profound human need for continuity and permanence, and by passing into common speech. Words and phrases from this liturgy have become part of the heritage of the English language by continuous reiteration over the centuries in public worship and in private devotion. In Church of England day schools pupils used to learn by heart the great Collects from the Prayer Book. That learning, together with regular church services where the Prayer Book was the only rite, had a genuine influence on the minds and imaginations of ordinary men and women. Though their own speech could not command the cadences and rhythms of Cranmer's prayers, because they were familiar with them they remembered them. My own experience of constant reiteration in Church has confirmed to me that as one gets older the essential poetry of this great liturgy has an ever more resonant meaning.

At home, abroad, in hospitals, on battlefields, in solitude, in society, in trouble and in prosperity, these words were remembered and gave comfort and hope in the great crises of innumerable human lives. The power and majesty of the language of the Book of Common Prayer were such that, in the words of one Collect, "Among the sundry and manifold changes of the world, our hearts may surely there be fixed where true joys are to be found".

I hope very much that this book will provide a new incentive to study the Collects and may even encourage people of all ages to commit some of them to memory. I have been delighted to see a revival in recent years of the learning by heart of passages from the Book of Common Prayer, spurred on in part by the annual Cranmer Awards arranged by the Prayer Book Society. There is no doubt in my own mind about the importance of the trend, since I do believe so strongly that the survival of the Book of Common Prayer is a touchstone of our ability as a society to value its spiritual roots, its liturgical continuity and its very identity as a nation of believers.

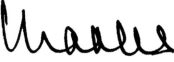

# INTRODUCTION

*"And now I come to the great thing which so much troubleth my conscience, more than anything that ever I did or said in my whole life: and that is, the setting abroad of writings contrary to the truth, which now I here renounce and refuse . . . and written for fear of death and to save my life, if it might be. . . ."*

The scene was the University church in Oxford. Thomas Cranmer, lately Archbishop of Canterbury, stood on a wretched platform opposite the pulpit, addressing the astounded congregation. He was in bare and ragged gown, his long grey beard touching his belt, a dirty old square cap on his head, passion in his voice. He had broken from his prepared text and spoke from the heart in this, his last public utterance before facing a terrible and fiery death.

*". . . and that is, all such bills and papers which I have written or signed with my hand – "*

He held it up, over his head.

*". . . since my degradation. And foreasmuch as my hand offended, writing contrary to my heart, my hand shall first be punished therefor: for, may I come to the fire, it shall be first burned."*

Those listening in the packed nave cried out in appeal to him to remember his recent recantation, read out earlier in his discourse, of Anglican doctrine in favour of Papal authority. This was the issue, at the very pivot of the Reformation, on which he had wavered agonisingly back and forth in seven varying recantations since Bloody Mary had succeeded to the throne three years before, and for which he had been deposed as Archbishop.

Ignoring the shouts, he almost leaped from the platform and thrust his way through to the South door, his guard pursuing him. Hurrying outside, he literally ran through the driving rain towards the place of execution in The Broad, so fast that his guard could barely keep up with him

As Spanish friars exhorted him in the name of the Catholic Queen and the Pope to recant once more, he was chained to the stake, the piled faggots were lit and in no time the fire was licking around him searing his flesh with torments. But he thrust his right arm into the living flame, crying out *"This hand hath offended!"* – the hand that had signed the recantations he so bitterly regretted. He held it there, steadfast and immovable – except for one moment when he withdrew it quickly to wipe his streaming face. Within minutes, his hand turned black, bubbled and was consumed; and not long after, with a courage and steadfastness that moved all those watching to tears, he gave up the ghost. It was 21 March 1556; Cranmer was 67.

By far the greatest monument to this passionate, learned, enigmatic man, and to the convulsions then shaking England, was his greatest creation, the Book of Common Prayer. It is as central to our life on these islands as our cathedrals and our very language itself.

One can still go to Cranmer's study, the room in Lambeth Palace where he actually wrote, translated and compiled that most precious jewel of England. It adjoins the chapel, on the first floor and opening onto the N side of the sanctuary, like a very large box in the theatre.

It is not the untouched original due to a wartime bomb; but one can stand, very still, where he must have sat at his desk, pen in the same hand that was later so terribly consumed, and hear, as he must have heard, the sound of the eternal Thames slapping against the Palace walls not far away, and the grinding of passing boats – as, in his day, he would have heard the creak of oars and the cry of boatmen as well as the ceaseless water.

A most powerful awareness of water and of the sea – the sea imagery which pervades his work – is one of many reasons why his words have such a memorable impact on us. We are an island people. None of us is ever far from the sea, whether geographically or inside our heads, and Cranmer is always fully conscious of that. Our literature is soaked in brine, the North Sea wind blows through its topsails. Such images pervade his most glorious work with their disturbing and uncanny capacity to engrave themselves, not only on the mind, but on the heart.

The original Prayer Book was published in 1549; the present book marks the 450th anniversary of its appearance. Its immense achievement was to bring together, in crackling English when our language was at its vigorous prime, and in simple, common form, the enormously wide, fragmented variety of mediaeval services that had for so long split the nation diocese by diocese. The seven monastic offices in Latin, spread through the day, were brilliantly distilled into Matins and Evensong in the vernacular – in knife-edged words and glorious tumbling phrases which, together with the language of the Communion Service, irradiate and are interwoven into the very flesh of English today; so much so that those phrases are now used daily, without knowing their origin, by millions of people who have never darkened the door of any church in their lives.

As memorable are the Collects, the subject of this book, those tough, exquisite little prayer-gems of English, of spirituality and sense of the living presence of the Almighty.

For centuries our children have learned the Collects by heart – in the case of one school I knew of in the 1960s, pupils were not allowed to leave the precincts on a Sunday until they had mastered the day's Collect and repeated it from memory to their housemistress – finding, as they grew older, how much they teach about divine compassion and majesty, human need and human helplessness apart from God.

Why are the Collects so important? It is not merely a matter of their antiquity – though there is something very powerful about our using the self-same words as our forebears and as the saints and martyrs did in their hour of trial, in the classical world as much as under the Nazis. Nor is it their penetrating beauty and precision of language. Nor is it their symmetry of form, remarkable though that is. Even more important is the doctrine inspiring them – their exposition of the manifold divine attributes, and the manifestation of how sinful man can lay his needs and weakness before a righteous but infinitely merciful God.

Whatever the origin of the word "Collect", it describes a very ancient form of liturgical prayer. Five of the Prayer Book Collects date from Leo I, Bishop of Rome 440-461, twenty from Gelasius, Bishop of Rome 492-496, and twenty-seven from Gregory the Great, 590-604, who himself condensed and re-arranged earlier liturgies – indeed, he himself calls the Collects he co-ordinated "ancient". It is not impossible some may date from Christ's lifetime and have been written in the very dawn light of our faith.

They are characterised by brevity and concentration; they ask for one thing only, and that in the tersest language. Each one is based on a significant scriptural source, and each follows a set pattern of construction.

A complete Collect has five parts. First there is the address to God. Secondly comes a description of some property or attribute of God, extending the address by a relative clause relating to the petition about to be made. The third part is the petition itself, the heart of the prayer. Fourthly, the reason or purpose behind the petition. The Collect ends with the only Christian way of approach to God – the name of Jesus. There is a musical form and inevitability about it all; one half-consciously anticipates the pattern of syntax and meaning as if one were listening to a Bach fugue turned into words.

No one has done more for our understanding of these seminal short, tough prayers than Canon Henry James Burgess and much of the scholarship I am vainly trying to imply is my own in fact derives from his two splendid books on the subject, *Why Prayer Book Collects* and *A Prayer for all Seasons*. Born in 1908, his distinguished life as parish priest, Canon of Sheffield Cathedral and Director of Education of that diocese happily still continues, during which he has brought out nine books on various theological and related subjects. With great generosity he has donated the copyright of his two Prayer Book books to the Prayer Book Society as guardians of his opinion far into the next century.

His break-down of the thrust and historical origin of each separate Collect appears in the following pages.

When in Oxford a few years ago I often used to pass the spot where Cranmer met his death, while visiting a much-loved step-daughter when she was at Balliol reading Greats. I would reach out and touch the small commemorative stone set in the wall, as I passed it. It was just fifteen feet from this stone, on the actual execution site, that workmen digging a trench at the end of the last century found "a quantity of Ashes".

It is curious, but although this find was meticulously recorded, few twentieth century biographers of Cranmer mention it, even as a speculative footnote. Is it too fanciful to say that, perhaps, it is because this cannot be his memorial? – that his true memorial is, as Pericles said of others, that he is now "woven into the stuff of other men's lives"?

For I am certain that when I hear his words in a London taxi going down Regent Street while the driver explains he listens to Choral Evensong on the BBC every week, because he "finds something wonderful" about it; when I observe a girl kneeling at the sanctuary rail in front of me about to take Communion, caught up in the fervour of love he expresses; or when the self-declared atheist sub-postmaster of a neighbouring village is selling me stamps over the potato sacks but we are both actually more-than-half listening to Cranmer's haunting cadences from the radio left on at the back of the shop, suddenly stirring the spirit and imagination, that Thomas Cranmer is alive and well and living in England.

IAN CURTEIS

# THE ORIGIN AND CHARACTERISTICS
# OF THE COLLECTS

The meaning of the word collect seems to be uncertain. It derives from the Latin "collecta" – a gathering together. Some have pointed out that in the early church, a service of Christian worship was called "a gathering together" (c.f. the modern "meeting") especially where worshippers converged at a central "church" and there would be a prayer for the gathering together (oratio ad collectam). Others point out that in ancient service books the "secreta" was a prayer "by the minister to himself", whereas the "collecta" was one in which the assembly (collecta) was included. Thirdly, it has been claimed that the collect gathers together the teaching of the epistle and gospel, and certainly some Prayer Book collects serve to prepare the worshippers for the teaching of the Scriptures that follow.

Whatever the origin of the word, the collect is a very ancient form of liturgical prayer. Five of the Prayer Book collects date back to Leo I who was Bishop of Rome, A.D. 440-461; twenty to Gelasius, Bishop of Rome, A.D. 492496, and twenty-seven to Gregory the Great, A.D, 590-604, who condensed and rearranged the earlier liturgies. Dr Bisse, Preacher at the Rolls, in 1717 writes of Gregory: "To avoid the charge of novelty for which he was censured, he doubtless went back into the highest antiquity. He himself calls these collects ancient: and we have no reason to doubt but that some of them might be derived from the original liturgies of the first century when the Church was obliged to compose and to use set forms of service, whereof our Lord has left us a pattern in his own prayer." Dr Bisse goes on to point out that it was Gregory who in A.D. 597 sent Augustine to convert the English: "Since then this renowned Bishop . . . who taught us who to worship, taught us also how to worship, since he left us . . . for the most part the very same prayers that we use at this day, we ought to esteem and preserve them." It is indeed one of the glories of the Book of Common Prayer that it uses prayers uttered by martyrs and holy men and women in their hour of trial, and which men and women of faith have together offered to God over so many centuries.

There is, however, much more to the collects than their antiquity. As Charles Hole has said: "The general characteristic of the collect is brevity and concentration." Adrian Fortescue points out that it "asks for one thing and one thing only, and that in the tersest language". The Puritans were critical of both the brevity and the terseness, but brevity makes for simplicity of thought. It does not tax the memory as a long prayer is apt to do, and so assists concentration. Bishop Taylor Smith, former Chaplain-General, was chairing a meeting in which the opening prayer was over-long. When the prayer eventually ended, the Bishop said, "While our brother was leading in prayer my mind went back . . . " and he proceeded to tell what he had been thinking! Dr Bisse's answer to the Puritans was, "When any single request is offered up in a short collect, it is sealed by an Amen by all the people", and he argued that this enabled them to turn their thoughts to another subject for prayer. He asserted: "All long prayers, however well composed, are weakened and injured according to their length."

Antiquity and brevity, however, are less important than the content of a prayer. That is why the third characteristic of the collect is so significant, for all the collects are scriptural. That this is the case is clearly demonstrated in Bailey's *The Liturgy compared with the Bible* which provides scriptural references for each section of every collect. It was to be expected that the compositions of our English Reformers would be Bible-based, as indeed they are, but the older collects also abound in allusions, sometimes indirect, to verses of the Bible. For example, the morning collect for peace with its clause, "in knowledge of whom standeth our eternal life" recalls Our Lord's words, "this is life eternal that they may know thee", and Trinity 19 "forasmuch as without thee we are not able to please thee" recalls His words "Without me ye can do nothing".

The fourth characteristic of the collect, its formal structure, requires a chapter to itself.

## THE STRUCTURE AND CONTENT
## OF THE COLLECTS

A complete collect has five parts. First, there is the address to God. Secondly, comes a description of some property or attribute of God, extending the address by a relative clause, defining a divine activity or attitude pertinent to the petition about to be made. Sometimes, instead, there is an acknowledgment of human error, weakness or unworthiness. Thirdly, there is the petition itself, the heart of the prayer. Fourthly, usually but not invariably, comes the reason for, or purpose behind, the petition. The collect ends with the only Christian way of approach to God – the name of Jesus Christ.

Before examining these parts in detail, it is important to note that the collect follows our Lord's own pattern prayer in being concerned first with the God to whom we come, and only then with the need we lay before Him. "When ye pray, say, Our Father which art in heaven, Hallowed be thy name." As in the Lord's Prayer, so in the collects. Nearly all start with an address to God: "Almighty God", "Almighty and everlasting God" or, more briefly, "O God" or "O Lord" are the most frequent – and then, as in the Lord's Prayer, there usually follows a relative clause beginning with "Who" which describes some particular divine attribute. The vision of God's grace or power resulting from this description becomes the ground, both for the nature of the petition about to be made, and for assurance that it will be accepted. To quote Dr Bisse: "In the standing collects for the daily service (i.e. Matins), when we pray for peace we invoke God as 'the author of peace and lover of accord'; when for protection, as 'almighty and everlasting God'; when for the sovereign, as 'king of kings and lord of lords'." Similarly when, on the second Sunday in Advent we pray for a right approach to the Bible, we begin, "Blessed Lord, who has caused all holy Scriptures to be written for our learning" when, on the third Sunday after Epiphany we speak of our infirmities and dangers, we begin "Almighty and everlasting God" when on Quinquagesima we seek the first fruit of the Spirit (love, Gr. Agape), we come to the God "who has taught us that all our doings without charity (Gr. Agape) are nothing worth".

Admittedly, there is not always this explicit connection between the divine attribute and the human petition, but this does not destroy the value of the collect's introduction to prayer. To quote Dr Bisse: "In some few collects the divine attribute mentioned has no direct reference to the matter of the petition, yet it always serves to strengthen the faith of the petitioner. For instance, suppose it were God's goodness as 'O most gracious God': or His power as 'O Almighty God': do not both these serve to strengthen our hopes of acceptance, whatever our petition be? God's goodness, by certifying that He is willing to help us: His power, by certifying that He is able to do it? And thus the preface to our Lord's prayer relates, not to the particular petitions contained in it, but rather to all prayer in general: intimating to us God's readiness to hear us, whatever we ask, because He is 'Our Father': and His ability to grant it, because He is 'in heaven'. " in short, the important thing about the pattern both of the Lord's Prayer and the collects is that they begin with unhurried contemplation of the kind of God to Whom we are praying, and only then move on to the petition we make. Bishop Dowden claims. "It is not too much to say that from the preambles to the collects, a full systematic statement of Christian truth, as to the Divine Nature and relations to man might be drawn out."

The petitions, however, are the heart of the collects. They are wonderfully varied, while their themes are markedly spiritual, and only incidentally material. In them we pray for:

| | |
|---|---|
| **Advent 1** | grace, |
| **Advent 2** | understanding of God's word, |
| **Advent 3** | preparedness for judgment, |
| **Advent 4** | freedom from the fetters of sin, |
| **Christmas Day** | new birth, |
| **The Circumcision** | obedience, |
| **Epiphany** | heavenly bliss |
| **Epiphany 1** | spiritual insight and consistent conduct, |
| **Epiphany 2** | peace of heart, |
| **Epiphany 3** | God's help and defence |
| **Epiphany 4** | strength to overcome danger and temptation, |
| **Epiphany 5** | true religion, |
| **Epiphany 6** | purity of character, |
| **Septuagesima** | divine deliverance, |
| **Sexagesima** | power in adversity, |
| **Quinquagesima** | the first fruit of the Holy Spirit, |
| **Ash Wednesday** | new and contrite hearts, |
| **Lent 1** | righteousness and true holiness, |

| | |
|---|---|
| **Lent 2** | bodily and spiritual health, |
| **Lent 3** | defence against enemies, |
| **Lent 4** | relief after confession of sin, |
| **Lent 5** | physical and spiritual preservation, |
| **Lent 6** | readiness to follow Christ in his sufferings and to share in his resurrection, |
| **Good Friday** | divine graciousness in the light of the Cross of Christ, |
| **Easter** | ability to achieve, by God's grace, the good we intend, |
| **Easter 1** | pure living and true service, |
| **Easter 2** | a gratitude which leads to a Christ-like life, |
| **Easter 3** | right belief begetting Christian conduct |
| **Easter 4** | hearts which have learned the secret of true joy |
| **Easter 5** | thoughts and conduct which God alone can inspire, |
| **Ascension** | hearts set upon the eternal |
| **Ascension 1** | a fresh experience of the Holy Spirit, |
| **Whitsun** | right judgment and spiritual strength, |
| **Trinity** | steadfast continuance in the true faith, |
| **Trinity 1** | grace to obey God's commandments, |
| **Trinity 2** | God-fearing love, |
| **Trinity 3** | defence in adversity, |
| **Trinity 4** | guidance through life here to life hereafter, |
| **Trinity 5** | peaceful and joyous service, |
| **Trinity 6** | love of God and experience of His promised bliss, |
| **Trinity 7** | increased devotion and strengthened character, |
| **Trinity 8** | providential government, |
| **Trinity 9** | divine enabling for right living, |
| **Trinity 10** | a divinely guided prayer life |
| **Trinity 11** | obedience leading to eternal bliss, |
| **Trinity 12** | Divine mercy and blessing, |
| **Trinity 13** | faithful service here and entrance into heaven hereafter, |
| **Trinity 14** | an increase of faith, hope and charity resulting in prayer pleasing to God, |
| **Trinity 15** | guidance to things profitable to our souls, |
| **Trinity 16** | the cleansing and defence of the Church of God, |
| **Trinity 17** | grace producing consistent conduct |
| **Trinity 18** | power to withstand the trinity of evil, |
| **Trinity 19** | the Holy Spirit's guidance and governance, |
| **Trinity 20** | cheerful obedience to God's will |
| **Trinity 21** | pardon, peace, cleansing and tranquil service, |
| **Trinity 22** | a godly Church devoutly serving the Lord and bringing Him glory, |
| **Trinity 23** | answered prayer, |
| **Trinity 24** | deliverance from sin |
| **Trinity 25** | wills stirred to bring forth the fruits of good works. |

The collects for Saints' days and collects following the communion service widen the scope of petition yet further, and it is no wonder Dr Bisse can claim, "There is no outward good nor inward grace, nothing that is fitting or necessary either for the body or the soul, either for ourselves or others, but may be prayed for in some particular and very pertinent collect."

Scripture is clear that prayer is not just a matter of demanding the right things from God. True prayer takes account of the warning by Our Lord's brother when he writes, "Ye ask, and receive not because ye ask amiss that ye may consume it upon your lusts" (James 4 v 3) or NIV, "When you ask, you do not receive because you ask with wrong motives that you may spend what you get on your pleasures." So the fourth part of the collect ensures that the motives are right. Thus, throughout Advent we seek grace to banish the works of darkness and to put on the armour of light "that in the last day when Christ shall come in his glorious majesty, to judge both the quick and the dead, we may rise to the life immortal". Likewise, in Advent 2 we pray for a right attitude to God's Word that by that Word "we may embrace and ever hold fast the blessed hope of everlasting life". On Ash Wednesday we lament our sins and pray "that we may obtain of thee, the God of all mercy, perfect remission and forgiveness". Every Sunday morning we pray for God's defence from sin and danger "that all our doings may be ordered by thy governance, to do always that is righteous in thy sight". Every Sunday evening we seek divinely given peace for two reasons (a) "that our hearts may be set to obey thy commandments" and (b) "that we may pass our time in rest and quietness".

This part, expressing the reason or purpose behind the petition, is absent from many of the collects: but where it is absent, it will usually be the case that the petition itself reveals the motive. Thus at Epiphany we ask that we "may after this life have the fruition (enjoyment: Latin fruor 'I enjoy') of thy glorious Godhead", and at Epiphany 1 God's people ask "that they may both perceive and know what things they ought to do, and also may have grace and power faithfully to fulfil the same".

Finally, just as all but four of the collects are addressed to God the Father – the exceptions being Advent 3, St Stephen, Lent 1 and Trinity – so they end, except in these four cases, with "through Jesus Christ our Lord" or with a like phrase. This universal ending accords with the words of our Lord reported in John 14 v 6 and John 16 v 23. Whereas Jews and Moslems, as well as Christians, pray to the sovereign God of the universe, the ending of the collect defines the Christian approach to God, and unites the worshipper with Him "who ever liveth to make intercession for us" (Hebrews 7 v 25).

## THE TEACHING OF THE COLLECTS

In *The Spirit of the Liturgy* R. Guardini points out that the prayers of the liturgy are governed by, and interwoven with, dogma. Reference has been made to the way in which the opening words of each collect – the address to God and the relative clause following it – together constitute a profound and moving description of the God we worship and, in some cases, an acknowledgment of human error, weakness or unworthiness.

To examine the teaching reflected in the complete collects, it is essential first to refer to church history. Some of the twenty collects taken from the sacramentary of Gelasius reflect the battle against Pelagianism. Pelagius stressed human free-will in such a way as to question the need of divine grace to guide and empower the will. His great opponent Augustine of Hippo, taught the soul's utter dependence on God's grace and Augustine's teaching is evident in the Gelasian collects. Thus the collect for Trinity 1 addresses God as "the strength of all them that put their trust in thee", and prays "grant us the help of thy grace that in keeping of thy commandments we may please thee both in will and deed". Trinity 9 likewise acknowledges "that we cannot do anything that is good without thee". In similar vein, the second collect at Evening Prayer begins "O God from whom all holy desires, all good counsels, and all just works do proceed".

Augustinian doctrine is also revealed in some of the twenty-seven collects from the sacramentary of Gregory the Great. The Sexagesima collect says that God sees "that we put not our trust in any thing we do", and Lent 2 similarly says that God sees "that we have no power of ourselves to help ourselves". Easter 4 says God "alone canst order the unruly wills and affections of sinful men".

The influence of Augustine is present in another way. The collects do not explicitly refer to his teaching on predestination, but some teach very clearly the doctrine of the Prevenience of God. Our word "prevent" has changed its meaning. By derivation it meant "come before", and the collects use it to seek prevenient grace. The prayers that follow the Communion are known as "Table Prayers". The best known of these Table Prayers begins "Prevent us O Lord, in all our doings" and the Easter collect has "as by thy special grace preventing us thou doest put into our minds good desires". In Trinity 17 we ask that God's grace "may always prevent and follow us". Even Christian people tend to forget that our relationship with God originates in His grace, and not in our efforts. We love God because He first loved us (1 John 4 v 19), and we need these collects to remind us that God is the true inspirer of our highest seeking and noblest endeavour. As Von Hugel has written "He secretly initiates what He openly crowns".

The collects speak of God's grace and power as able to meet man's need in a threefold way: (a) by God's Word written; (b) by the Word made flesh; (c) by the work of the Holy Spirit.

*(a) God's Word written:* Advent 2 describes the divine origin and purpose of Holy Scripture and tells how attention to, and response to, the Word of God leads to the sure hope of eternal life. One of the post-communion collects describes how, when "through God's grace" the word is "grafted inwardly in our hearts", it "brings forth in us the fruit of good living". The theme of the Quinquagesima collect on Christian love is based on 1 Corinthians 13. On St Bartholomew's day, the collect – which can be traced back to the early 5th century – sets out the characteristic of a true apostle, as one

who believes God's Word and is commissioned to preach it, and it prays that likewise the Church may love that word, preach it and receive it. How needful is that prayer today!

*(b) The Word made flesh:* Equally noteworthy are the collects witnessing to the incarnation, perfect life, atoning death, and mighty resurrection of Jesus Christ, and to the need for a right relationship to Him. At Christmas, as we remember His birth, we pray that new birth as children of God may be ours. Thus He who was born in Bethlehem may be born in our hearts. So, too, eight days later, His circumcision finds its parallel in our experiencing "true circumcision of the Spirit", and so learning complete obedience to God's will. Epiphany 6 declares a two-fold purpose of Christ's incarnation – to destroy sin's power and to make us God's sons and heirs of eternal life – and prays that our response may be Christ-likeness of character in preparation for His coming again. On the Sunday before Easter the epistle is Paul's account of the incarnation, stressing Christ's humility in becoming man and dying for men, and he begins with the bidding "Let this mind be in you which, was also in Christ Jesus". The collect echoes the apostolic bidding as we pray that we may follow His example in facing suffering and in resurrection.

Similarly, Easter 2 gives thanks both for His sacrificial death for sin and for His perfect life, and prays that we may thankfully accept what by His death He has done for us, thereby enabling us to follow the example set by His life.

*(c) The Work of the Holy Spirit:* At Quinquagesima the collect describes the Holy Spirit as the dynamo of Christian love, and on Good Friday the Spirit is the sanctifier of the Church. At Whitsun the Spirit is the author of "right judgement in all things" and the provider of "holy comfort", and in the collect of Trinity 19 it is He who can "direct and rule our hearts".

Thus, as they follow the Church's year, the collects provide a compendium of Christian doctrine enabling the worshipper, as he prays, to enter into all the wonder of divine redemption, and to know in heart and mind God's gracious purposes "for us men and for our salvation". Furthermore, those purposes are certain of fulfilment because of the divine providence.

Thus, the collects teach us that God governs "all things in heaven and earth" (Epiphany 2), that His "never-failing providence ordereth all things both in heaven and earth" (Trinity 8), and therefore we can with assurance pray "Keep us we beseech thee under the protection of thy good providence" (Trinity 2). Surely Joseph Hart was mindful of these collects when he wrote:

> This, this is the God we adore,
> Our faithful unchangeable friend
> Whose love is as great as His power
> And neither knows measure nor end.

The sheer beauty of the 1662 collects, their rhythmic balance, their majestic sense of God, their reverence of approach and deep theological content make them indeed what Professor Martin calls "small pattern prayers, tiny flights of intimate devotion". They manifest, as Hebert says, "the genius of liturgy", and they pass Evelyn Underhill's test of true liturgical language – "one which enchants and informs, evoking moments of awe and love which no exhortation can obtain". The Prayer Book collects constitute one of the glories of Anglican worship, not least because, as the Australian Barry Spurr has so well put it, "In Cranmer's collects, rich in metaphor, succinct without brusqueness, we find quite simply inspired speech". Surely, all who believe that true liturgy should enable us to worship the Lord in the beauty of holiness, should unite to restore them to universal use.

# ORIGIN OR AUTHORSHIP
## OF EACH COLLECT
### I . The Collects at Morning and Evening Prayer

These four collects all originated in the Sacramentary of Gelasius and were incorporated in the Sarum Breviary, from which in 1549 Cranmer translated them.

### 2. The Sunday Collects

Most of these originated in the Sacramentaries of either: (a) Leo I (Bishop of Rome in the early 5th century A.D.) or (b) Gelasius (Bishop of Rome in the late 5th century A.D.) or (c) Gregory (Bishop of Rome in the late 6th century A.D.). They were incorporated in the Sarum Missal, and were translated in 1549, most of them by Cranmer. The earliest known form is given in the following list, whether or not a later Sacramentary contained it or amended it.

| | |
|---|---|
| **Advent 1** | 1549. Probably composed by Cranmer. (The Sarum Missal collect for Advent I resembled more the B.C.P. collect for Advent 4.) |
| **Advent 2** | 1549. Probably composed by Cranmer. |
| **Advent 3** | 1662. Probably composed by Bishop Cosin. (It replaced the translation from the Sarum Missal in use from 1549.) |
| **Advent 4** | Gelasius. Revised 1662. |
| **Christmas** | 1549. Probably composed by Cranmer. |
| **St Stephen** | Gregory. Bishop Cosin enlarged version of 1549 was adopted in 1662. |
| **St John the Evangelist** | Gelasius, but expanded in 1549 and again in 1662. |
| **The Innocents** | Gelasius 1549, but re-written in 1662. |
| **The Circumcision** | Composed 1549, but partly based on a "Benediction on the Octave of the Lord" in Gregory. |
| **The Epiphany** | 1549. Gregory. |
| **Epiphany 1** | 1549. Gregory. |
| **Epiphany 2** | 1549. Gregory. Slightly altered in 1662. |
| **Epiphany 3** | 1549. Gregory (but modified). |
| **Epiphany 4** | 1549. Gregory (but varied in 1549, and much altered in |

| | |
|---|---|
| | 1662). |
| **Epiphany 5** | 1549. Gregory (very freely translated) . |
| **Epiphany 6** | 1662. Composed by Bishop Cosin. |
| **Septuagesima** | 1549. Gregory (but doctrine safeguarded by adding "By Thy goodness"). |
| **Sexagesima** | 1549. Gregory (but amended in translation). |
| **Quinquagesima** | 1549. Probably composed by Cranmer. |
| **Ash Wednesday** | 1549. Probably by Cranmer, using a thought from the Sarum collect. |
| **Lent 1** | 1549. Probably composed by Cranmer. |
| **Lent 2** | 1549. Gregory, but very free translation. |
| **Lent 3** | 1549. Gregory. |
| **Lent 4** | 1549. Gregory. Slightly altered in 1662. |
| **Lent 5** | 1549. Gregory freely translated. |
| **Lent 6** | 1549. Gelasius, but translation made specific reference to the death on the Cross by adding "of thy tender love towards mankind". |
| **Good Friday** | 1st Collect 1549. Gregory. |
| | 2nd Collect 1549. Gelasius. |
| | 3rd Collect 1549. Ideas collected from three collects of Gelasius and Gregory. |
| **Easter Even** | 1662. Probably by Laud, but reconstructed by Cosin. |
| **Easter** | 1549. Gelasius. |
| **Easter 1** | Composed 1549, and made the collect for Easter 1 in 1662. |
| **Easter 2** | Composed 1549. |
| **Easter 3** | 1549. Leo I . |
| **Easter 4** | 1549. Gelasius. In 1662 the relative clause was amended to "who alone canst order the unruly wills and affections of sinful men". |
| **Easter 5** | 1549. Gelasius. |
| **Ascension** | 1549. A free translation from Gelasius. |
| **Ascension 1** | 1549. The author used part of Vespers in the Sarum Breviary. |
| **Whitsunday** | 1549. Gregory. |
| **Trinity** | 1549. Gregory. Slightly amended in 1662. |
| **Trinity 1** | 1549. Gelasius. Slightly altered in 1662. |
| **Trinity 2** | Freely translated in 1549 from Gelasius and reshaped in 1662. |
| **Trinity 3** | 1549. Gelasius: a free translation. Enlarged in 1662 by the phrase "and comforted in all dangers and adversities". |
| **Trinity 4** | 1549. Gregory. |
| **Trinity 5** | 1549. Leo I. |
| **Trinity 6** | Gelasius. The original had "in all things and above all |

| | |
|---|---|
| | things" translated in 1549 as "in all things", while the 1662 version is "above all things". |
| **Trinity 7** | 1549. Gelasius, but freely translated, and thereby much improved. |
| **Trinity 8** | 1549. Gelasius. Much improved in 1662 by a freer translation. |
| **Trinity 9** | 1549. Leo I. Amended in 1662. |
| **Trinity 10** | 1549. Leo I, but a marked improvement on the Latin original. |
| **Trinity 11** | 1549. Gelasius. In 1662 "running the way of Thy commandments" was substituted for the English and Latin "running to Thy promises". |
| **Trinity 12** | 1549. Leo I. The English version in 1549 and 1662 enriched the Latin original. |
| **Trinity 13** | Leo I, but the 1549 translation doctrinally improved the original, and there was a further slight amendment in 1662. |
| **Trinity 14** | Leo I. The 1549 translation replaced "deserve to obtain" by "obtain". |
| **Trinity 15** | Gelasius, but, doctrinally improved by the 1549 translation. |
| **Trinity 16** | Gelasius, but the 1549 collect was a free translation. |
| **Trinity 17** | 1549. Gregory. |
| **Trinity 18** | 1549. Gelasius. The original "avoid the infections of the devil" became in 1662 "withstand the temptations of the world, the flesh and the devil". |
| **Trinity 19** | Gelasius, but reshaped in 1549 and further improved in 1662. |
| **Trinity 20** | 1549. Gelasius, but a free translation. In 1662 "cheerfully" replaced the original Latin (and 1549 English) " with free hearts". |
| **Trinity 21** | 1549. Gelasius, but a free translation. |
| **Trinity 22** | 1549. From the Anglo-Saxon missal of Leofric of Exeter A.D. 1050. |
| **Trinity 23** | 1549. Gregory, but a free translation. |
| **Trinity 24** | 1549. Gregory. |
| **Trinity 25** | 1549. Gregory, but less of a translation than a reinterpretation. |

### 3. Saints' Days Collects

Apart from that for St Andrew's Day, most of these were composed in 1549 mainly by Cranmer, but a few were free translations from the early Sacramentaries via the Sarum Missal.

| | |
|---|---|
| **St Andrew** | The Prayer Book of 1552 introduced this new collect to replace that of 1549 which assumed that St Andrew met a martyr's death. |
| **St Thomas** | 1549. |
| **St Paul** | A free translation from Gregory in 1549 was greatly improved in 1662. |
| **The Presentation** | 1549. Gregory. A free translation amended in 1662. |
| **St Matthias** | 1549. |
| **The Annunciation** | 1549. An exact translation of the Sarum Missal post-communion collect. |
| **St Mark** | 1549. In 1662 "so to be established . . . that we be not, like children" became "that being not like children . . . we may be established". |
| **St Philip & St James** | 1549. Enlarged in 1662. |
| **St Barnabas** | 1549. |
| **St John Baptist** | 1549. |
| **St Peter** | 1549. |
| **St James** | 1549. |
| **St Bartholomew** | Gregory, but much altered 1549. |
| **St Matthew** | 1549, but "The Apostle" added 1662. |
| **St Michael & All Angels** | 1549. Gregory. |
| **St Luke** | 1549. |
| **St Simon & St Jude** | 1549. |
| **All Saints** | 1549. |

4. The Lord's Supper or Holy Communion

**Collect for Purity**, 1549. Translated from the Sarum Missal, and believed to be the work of the Anglo-Saxon Bishop Alcuin.

**The Table Prayers** (Collects after the Communion Service).

"Assist us mercifully . . .", 1549. Gelasius. A lovely adaptation of a Sarum collect for travellers.

"O Almighty Lord . . . ", 1549. Gregory doctrinally revised, it is the translation of a prayer which followed the Sarum service of Prime.

"Grant we beseech Thee . . .". Composed in 1549.

"Prevent us O Lord . . .", 1549. Gregory.

"Almighty God, the fountain . . . " . Composed in 1549.

"Almighty God, who has promised . . .". Composed in 1549.

General Note. That many collects were slightly altered, and generally (though not always) improved, in 1662, and that the significant changes were comparatively few, indicates the painstaking care and thoroughness of the Restoration revisers.

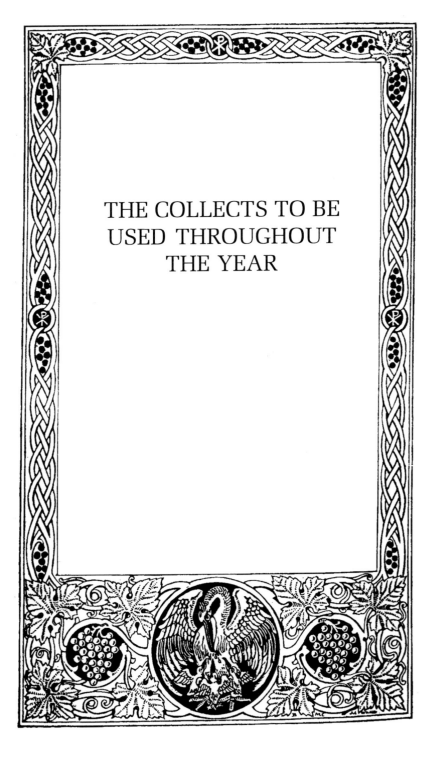

THE COLLECTS TO BE
USED THROUGHOUT
THE YEAR

# MORNING PRAYER

## THE COLLECT OF THE DAY

*The Second Collect, for Peace.*

O GOD, who art the author of peace and lover of concord, in knowledge of whom standeth our eternal life, whose service is perfect freedom: Defend us thy humble servants in all assaults of our enemies; that we, surely trusting in thy defence, may not fear the power of any adversaries; through the might of Jesus Christ our Lord.                    *Amen.*

*The Third Collect, for Grace.*

O LORD our heavenly Father, Almighty and everlasting God, who hast safely brought us to the beginning of this day: Defend us in the same with thy mighty power; and grant that this day we fall into no sin, neither run into any kind of danger; but that all our doings may be ordered by thy governance, to do always that is righteous in thy sight; through Jesus Christ our Lord.            *Amen.*

# EVENING PRAYER

## THE COLLECT OF THE DAY

*The Second Collect at Evening Prayer.*

O GOD, from whom all holy desires, all good coun-sels, and all just works do proceed: Give unto thy servants that peace which the world cannot give; that both our hearts may be set to obey thy commandments, and also that by thee we being defended from the fear of our enemies may pass our time in rest and quietness; through the merits of Jesus Christ our Saviour.              *Amen.*

*The Third Collect, for Aid against all Perils.*

L IGHTEN our darkness, we beseech thee, O Lord; and by thy great mercy defend us from all perils and dangers of this night; for the love of thy only Son, our Saviour Jesus Christ.              *Amen.*

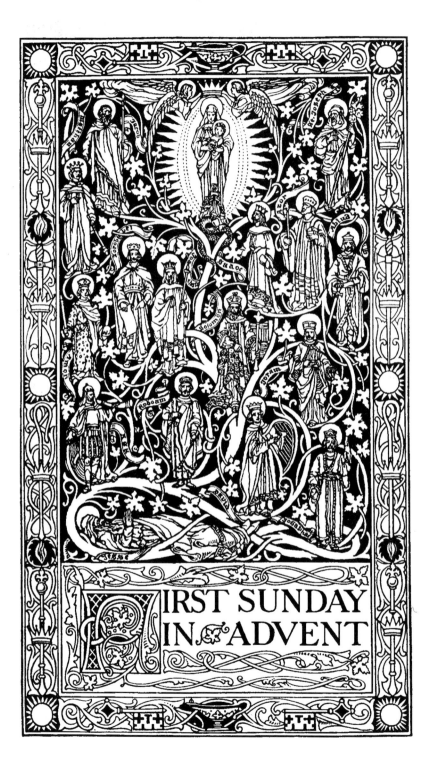

FIRST SUNDAY
IN ADVENT

### THE FIRST SUNDAY IN ADVENT

ALMIGHTY God, give us grace that we may cast away the works of darkness, and put upon us the armour of light, now in the time of this mortal life, in which thy Son Jesus Christ came to visit us in great humility; that in the last day, when he shall come again in his glorious Majesty, to judge both the quick and the dead, we may rise to the life immortal; through him who liveth and reigneth with thee and the Holy Ghost, now and ever.     *Amen.*

### THE SECOND SUNDAY IN ADVENT

BLESSED Lord, who hast caused all holy Scriptures to be written for our learning: Grant that we may in such wise hear them, read, mark, learn, and inwardly digest them, that by patience and comfort of thy holy Word, we may embrace and ever hold fast the blessed hope of everlasting life, which thou hast given us in our Saviour Jesus Christ. *Amen.*

### THE THIRD SUNDAY IN ADVENT

LORD Jesu Christ, who at thy first coming didst send thy messenger to prepare thy way before thee: Grant that the ministers and stewards of thy mysteries may likewise so prepare and make ready thy way, by turning the hearts of the disobedient to the wisdom of the just, that at thy second coming to judge the world we may be found an acceptable people in thy sight, who livest and reignest with the Father and the Holy Spirit, ever one God, world without end.     *Amen.*

O Sapientia     O Adonai     O Clavis

## THE FOURTH SUNDAY IN ADVENT

O LORD, raise up (we pray thee) thy power, and come among us, and with great might succour us; that whereas, through our sins and wickedness, we are sore let and hindered in running the race that is set before us, thy bountiful grace and mercy may speedily help and deliver us; through the satisfaction of thy Son our Lord, to whom with thee and the Holy Ghost be honour and glory, world without end. *Amen.*

O Pastor     O Rex     O Emmanuel     O Oriens

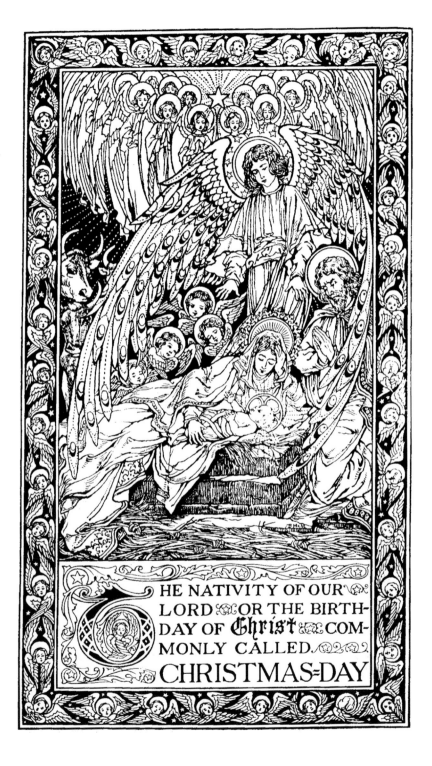

THE NATIVITY OF OUR LORD, OR THE BIRTH-DAY OF Christ, COMMONLY CALLED, CHRISTMAS=DAY

# CHRISTMAS DAY
## December 25

ALMIGHTY God, who hast given us thy only-begotten Son to take our nature upon him, and as at this time to be born of a pure Virgin: Grant that we being regenerate, and made thy children by adoption and grace, may daily be renewed by thy Holy Spirit; through the same our Lord Jesus Christ, who liveth and reigneth with thee and the same Spirit, ever one God, world without end. *Amen.*

.... Glory to God in the highest ....
and on Earth peace . goodwill toward men

## SAINT STEPHEN'S DAY
### December 26

GRANT, O Lord, that in all our sufferings here upon earth, for the testimony of thy truth, we may steadfastly look up to heaven, and by faith behold the glory that shall be revealed; and, being filled with the Holy Ghost, may learn to love and bless our persecutors, by the example of thy first Martyr Saint Stephen, who prayed for his murderers to thee, O blessed Jesus, who standest at the right hand of God to succour all those that suffer for thee, our only Mediator and Advocate. *Amen.*

## SAINT JOHN
## THE EVANGELIST'S DAY
### December 27

MERCIFUL Lord, we beseech thee to cast thy bright beams of light upon thy Church, that it being enlightened by the doctrine of thy blessed Apostle and Evangelist Saint John may so walk in the light of thy truth, that it may at length attain to the light of everlasting life; through Jesus Christ our Lord. *Amen.*

Saint Stephen

Saint John
the Evangelist

## THE INNOCENTS' DAY
### December 28

O ALMIGHTY God, who out of the mouths of
babes  and sucklings hast ordained strength,
and madest infants to glorify thee by their deaths:
Mortify and kill all vices in us, and so strengthen us
by thy grace, that by the innocency of our lives, and
constancy of our faith, even unto death, we may
glorify thy holy Name; through Jesus Christ our Lord.

*Amen.*

The
Innocents Day

## THE SUNDAY AFTER
## CHRISTMAS DAY

ALMIGHTY God, who hast given us thy onlybegotten Son to take our nature upon him, and as at this time to be born of a pure Virgin: Grant that we being regenerate, and made thy children by adoption and grace, may daily be renewed by thy Holy Spirit; through the same our Lord Jesus Christ, who liveth and reigneth with thee and the same Spirit, ever one God, world without end.    *Amen.*

## NEW YEAR'S DAY
### AND
## THE CIRCUMCISION OF CHRIST

ALMIGHTY God, who madest thy blessed Son to be circumcised, and obedient to the law for man: Grant us the true circumcision of the Spirit; that, our hearts, and all our members, being mortified from all worldly and carnal lusts, we may in all things obey thy blessed will; through the same thy Son Jesus Christ our Lord.    *Amen.*

The Circumcision of
Christ

The EPIPHANY OR THE MANIFESTATION OF Christ TO THE GENTILES.

## THE EPIPHANY
## OR
## THE MANIFESTATION OF CHRIST TO THE
## GENTILES
### January 6

O GOD, who by the leading of a star didst manifest thy only-begotten Son to the Gentiles: Mercifully grant, that we, which know thee now by faith, may after this life have the fruition of thy glorious Godhead; through Jesus Christ our Lord.  *Amen.*

## THE FIRST SUNDAY AFTER
## THE EPIPHANY

O LORD, we beseech thee mercifully to receive the prayers of thy people which call upon thee: and grant that they may both perceive and know what things they ought to do, and also may have grace and power faithfully to fulfil the same; through Jesus Christ our Lord.  *Amen.*

## THE SECOND SUNDAY AFTER
## THE EPIPHANY

A LMIGHTY and everlasting God, who dost govern all things in heaven and earth: Mercifully hear the supplications of thy people, and grant us thy peace all the days of our life; through Jesus Christ our Lord.  *Amen.*

## THE THIRD SUNDAY AFTER
## THE EPIPHANY

A LMIGHTY and everlasting God, mercifully look upon our infirmities, and in all our dangers and necessities stretch forth thy right hand to help and defend us; through Jesus Christ our Lord.  *Amen.*

## THE FOURTH SUNDAY AFTER
## THE EPIPHANY

O GOD, who knowest us to be set in the midst of so many and great dangers, that by reason of the frailty of our nature we cannot always stand upright: Grant to us such strength and protection, as may support us in all dangers, and carry us through all temptations; through Jesus Christ our Lord.

*Amen.*

## THE FIFTH SUNDAY AFTER
## THE EPIPHANY

O LORD, we beseech thee to keep thy Church and household continually in thy true religion; that they who do lean only upon the hope of thy heavenly grace may evermore be defended by thy mighty power; through Jesus Christ our Lord. *Amen.*

## THE SIXTH SUNDAY AFTER
## THE EPIPHANY

O GOD, whose blessed Son was manifested that he might destroy the works of the devil, and make us the sons of God, and heirs of eternal life: Grant us, we beseech thee, that, having this hope, we may purify. ourselves, even as he is pure; that, when he shall appear again with power and great glory, we may be made like unto him in his eternal and glorious kingdom; where with thee, O Father, and thee, O Holy Ghost, he liveth and reigneth, ever one God, world without end.

*Amen.*

## SEPTUAGESIMA
### OR THE THIRD SUNDAY BEFORE LENT

O LORD, we beseech thee favourably to hear the prayers of thy people; that we, who are justly punished for our offences, may be mercifully delivered by thy goodness, for the glory of thy Name; through Jesus Christ our Saviour, who liveth and reigneth with thee and the Holy Ghost, ever one God, world without end. *Amen.*

## SEXAGESIMA
### OR THE SECOND SUNDAY BEFORE LENT

O LORD God, who seest that we put not our trust in any thing that we do: Mercifully grant that by thy power we may be defended against all adversity; through Jesus Christ our Lord. *Amen.*

## QUINQUAGESIMA
### OR THE NEXT SUNDAY BEFORE LENT

O LORD, who has taught us that all our doings without charity are nothing worth: Send thy Holy Ghost, and pour into our hearts that most excellent gift of charity, the very bond of peace and of all virtues, without which whosoever liveth is counted dead before thee: Grant this for thine only Son Jesus Christ's sake. *Amen.*

## THE FIRST DAY OF LENT
COMMONLY CALLED
### ASH WEDNESDAY

ALMIGHTY and everlasting God, who hatest nothing that thou hast made, and dost forgive the sins of all them that are penitent: Create and make in us new and contrite hearts, that we worthily lamenting our sins, and acknowledging our wretchedness, may obtain of thee, the God of all mercy, perfect remission and forgiveness; through Jesus Christ our Lord.                    *Amen.*

## THE FIRST SUNDAY IN LENT

O LORD, who for our sake didst fast forty days and forty nights: Give us grace to use such abstinence, that, our flesh being subdued to the Spirit, we may ever obey thy godly motions in righteousness and true holiness, to thy honour and glory, who livest and reignest with the Father and the Holy Ghost, one God, world without end. *Amen.*

## THE SECOND SUNDAY IN LENT

ALMIGHTY God, who seest that we have no power of ourselves to help ourselves: Keep us both outwardly in our bodies, and inwardly in our souls; that we may be defended from all adversities which may happen to the body, and from all evil thoughts which may assault and hurt the soul; through Jesus Christ our Lord. *Amen.*

## THE THIRD SUNDAY IN LENT

WE beseech thee, Almighty God, look upon the hearty desires of thy humble servants, and stretch forth the right hand of thy Majesty, to be our defence against all our enemies; through Jesus Christ our Lord. *Amen.*

## THE FOURTH SUNDAY IN LENT

GRANT, we beseech thee, Almighty God, that we, who for our evil deeds do worthily deserve to be punished, by the comfort of thy grace may mercifully be relieved; through our Lord and Saviour Jesus Christ. *Amen.*

## THE FIFTH SUNDAY IN LENT
COMMONLY CALLED
### PASSION SUNDAY

WE beseech thee, Almighty God, mercifully to look upon thy people; that by thy great goodness they may be governed and preserved evermore, both in body and soul; through Jesus Christ our Lord. *Amen.*

## THE SUNDAY NEXT BEFORE EASTER
COMMONLY CALLED
### PALM SUNDAY

ALMIGHTY and everlasting God, who, of thy tender love towards mankind, hast sent thy Son our Saviour Jesus Christ, to take upon him our flesh, and to suffer death upon the cross, that all mankind should follow the example of his great humility: Mercifully grant, that we may both follow the example of his patience, and also be made partakers of his resurrection; through the same Jesus Christ our Lord. *Amen.*

GOOD FRIDAY

He sent him to Herod | I find no fault in him | When they had scourged him

## GOOD FRIDAY

ALMIGHTY God, we beseech thee graciously to behold this thy family, for which our Lord Jesus Christ was contented to be betrayed, and given up into the hands of wicked men, and to suffer death upon the cross, who now liveth and reigneth with thee and the Holy Ghost, ever one God, world without end. *Amen.*

ALMIGHTY and everlasting God, by whose Spirit the whole body of the Church is governed and sanctified: Receive our supplications and prayers, which we offer before thee for all estates of men in thy holy Church, that every member of the same, in his vocation and ministry, may truly and godly serve thee; through our Lord and Saviour Jesus Christ. *Amen.*

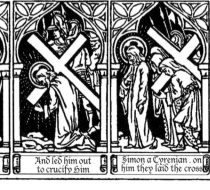

They clothed him with purple | And led him out to crucify him | Simon a Cyrenian . on him they laid the cross | There they . . . Crucified him

## GOOD FRIDAY

O MERCIFUL God, who hast made all men, and hatest nothing that thou hast made, nor wouldest the death of a sinner, but rather that he should be converted and live: Have mercy upon all Jews, Turks, Infidels, and Hereticks, and take from them all ignorance, hardness of heart, and contempt of thy word; and so fetch them home, blessed Lord, to thy flock, that they may be saved among the remnant of the true Israelites, and be made one fold under one shepherd, Jesus Christ our Lord, who liveth and reigneth with thee and the Holy Spirit, one God, world without end. *Amen.*

## EASTER EVEN

GRANT, O Lord, that as we are baptized into the death of thy blessed Son our Saviour Jesus Christ, so by continual mortifying our corrupt affections we may be buried with him; and that, through the grave, and gate of death, we may pass to our joyful resurrection; for his merits, who died, and was buried, and rose again for us, thy Son Jesus Christ our Lord. *Amen.*

When Joseph had taken the body

Laid it in his own new tomb

They went and made the sepulchre sure

## EASTER DAY

ALMIGHTY God, who through thine only-begotten Son Jesus Christ hast overcome death, and opened unto us the gate of everlasting life: We humbly beseech thee, that as by thy special grace preventing us thou dost put into our minds good desires, so by thy continual help we may bring the same to good effect; through Jesus Christ our Lord, who liveth and reigneth with thee and the Holy Ghost, ever one God, world without end. *Amen.*

Peter therefore went forth, and that other disciple, and came to the sepulchre

## THE FIRST SUNDAY AFTER EASTER
### COMMONLY CALLED
## LOW SUNDAY

ALMIGHTY Father, who hast given thine only Son to die for our sins, and to rise again for our justification: Grant us so to put away the leaven of malice and wickedness, that we may alway serve thee in pureness of living and truth; through the merits of the same thy Son Jesus Christ our Lord.

*Amen.*

## THE SECOND SUNDAY AFTER EASTER

ALMIGHTY God, who hast given thine only Son to be unto us both a sacrifice for sin, and also an example of godly life: Give us grace that we may always most thankfully receive that his inestimable benefit, and also daily endeavour ourselves to follow the blessed steps of his most holy life; through the same Jesus Christ our Lord.           *Amen.*

## THE THIRD SUNDAY AFTER EASTER

ALMIGHTY God, who shewest to them that be in error the light of thy truth, to the intent that they may return into the way of righteousness: Grant unto all them that are admitted into the fellowship of Christ's religion, that they may eschew those things that are contrary to their profession, and follow all such things as are agreeable to the same; through our Lord Jesus Christ.           *Amen.*

## THE FOURTH SUNDAY AFTER EASTER

O ALMIGHTY God, who alone canst order the unruly wills and affections of sinful men: Grant unto thy people, that they may love the thing which thou commandest, and desire that which thou dost promise; that so, among the sundry and manifold changes of the world, our hearts may surely there be fixed, where true joys are to be found; through Jesus Christ our Lord.          *Amen.*

## THE FIFTH SUNDAY AFTER EASTER
### COMMONLY CALLED
### ROGATION SUNDAY

O LORD, from whom all good things do come: Grant to us thy humble servants, that by thy holy inspiration we may think those things that be good, and by thy merciful guiding may perform the same; through our Lord Jesus Christ.          *Amen.*

ASCENSION DAY

## ASCENSION DAY

GRANT, we beseech thee, Almighty God, that like as we do believe thy only-begotten Son our Lord Jesus Christ to have ascended into the heavens; so we may also in heart and mind thither ascend, and with him continually dwell, who liveth and reigneth with thee and the Holy Ghost, one God, world without end. *Amen.*

## SUNDAY AFTER ASCENSION DAY

O GOD the King of glory, who hast exalted thine only Son Jesus Christ with great triumph unto thy kingdom in heaven: We beseech thee, leave us not comfortless; but send to us thine Holy Ghost to comfort us, and exalt us unto the same place whither our Saviour Christ is gone before, who liveth and reigneth with thee and the Holy Ghost, one God, world without end. *Amen.*

And while they looketh stedfastly toward heaven, as he went up behold, two men stood by them in white apparel

WHIT SUNDAY

The Spirit of Power     The Spirit of Riches     The Spirit of Wisdom

## WHITSUNDAY

GOD, who as at this time didst teach the hearts of thy faithful people, by the sending to them the light of thy Holy Spirit: Grant us by the same Spirit to have a right judgement in all things, and evermore to rejoice in his holy comfort; through the merits of Christ Jesus our Saviour, who liveth and reigneth with thee, in the unity of the same Spirit, one God, world without end. *Amen.*

The Spirit of Blessing     The Spirit of Glory     The Spirit of Honour     The Spirit of Strength

## TRINITY SUNDAY

ALMIGHTY and everlasting God, who hast given unto us thy servants grace, by the confession of a true faith, to acknowledge the glory of the eternal Trinity, and in the power of the Divine Majesty to worship the Unity: we beseech thee, that thou wouldest keep us steadfast in this faith, and evermore defend us from all adversities, who livest and reignest, one God, world without end.     *Amen.*

## THE FIRST SUNDAY AFTER TRINITY

O GOD, the strength of all them that put their trust in thee, mercifully accept our prayers; and because through the weakness of our mortal nature we can do no good thing without thee, grant us the help of thy grace, that in keeping of thy commandments we may please thee both in will and deed; through Jesus Christ our Lord.     *Amen.*

## THE SECOND SUNDAY AFTER TRINITY

O LORD, who never failest to help and govern them whom thou dost bring up in thy steadfast fear and love: Keep us, we beseech thee, under the protection of thy good providence, and make us to have a perpetual fear and love of thy holy name; through Jesus Christ our Lord.     *Amen.*

## THE THIRD SUNDAY AFTER TRINITY

O LORD, we beseech thee mercifully to hear us and grant that we, to whom thou hast given an hearty desire to pray, may by thy mighty aid be defended and comforted in all dangers and adversities; through Jesus Christ our Lord.     *Amen.*

### THE FOURTH SUNDAY AFTER TRINITY

O God, the protector of all that trust in thee, without whom nothing is strong, nothing is holy: Increase and multiply upon us thy mercy; that, thou being our ruler and guide, we may so pass through things temporal, that we finally lose not the things eternal: Grant this, O heavenly Father, for Jesus Christ's sake our Lord. *Amen.*

### THE FIFTH SUNDAY AFTER TRINITY

GRANT, O Lord, we beseech thee, that the course of this world may be so peaceably ordered by thy governanace, that thy Church may joyfully serve thee in all godly quietness; through Jesus Christ our Lord. *Amen.*

### THE SIXTH SUNDAY AFTER TRINITY

O GOD, who hast prepared for them that love thee such good things as pass man's understanding: Pour into our hearts such love toward thee, that we, loving thee above all things, may obtain thy promises, which exceed all that we can desire; through Jesus Christ our Lord. *Amen.*

### THE SEVENTH SUNDAY AFTER TRINITY

LORD of all power and might, who art the author and giver of all good things: Graft in our hearts the love of thy name, increase in us true religion, nourish us with all goodness, and of thy great mercy keep us in the same; through Jesus Christ our Lord. *Amen.*

### THE EIGHTH SUNDAY AFTER TRINITY

O GOD, whose never-failing providence ordereth all things both in heaven and earth: We humbly beseech thee to put away from us all hurtful things, and to give us those things which be profitable for us; through Jesus Christ our Lord. *Amen.*

## THE NINTH SUNDAY AFTER TRINITY

GRANT to us, Lord, we beseech thee, the spirit to think and do always such things as be rightful; that we, who cannot do any thing that is good without thee, may by thee be enabled to live according to thy will; through Jesus Christ our Lord.    *Amen.*

## THE TENTH SUNDAY AFTER TRINITY

LET thy merciful ears, O Lord, be open to the prayers of thy humble servants; and that they may obtain their petitions make them to ask such things as shall please thee; through Jesus Christ our Lord.                                    *Amen.*

## THE ELEVENTH SUNDAY AFTER TRINITY

O GOD, who declarest thy almighty power most chiefly in shewing mercy and pity: Mercifully grant unto us such a measure of thy grace, that we, running the way of thy commandments, may obtain thy gracious promises, and be made partakers of thy heavenly treasure; through Jesus Christ our Lord.
*Amen.*

## THE TWELFTH SUNDAY AFTER TRINITY

ALMIGHTY and everlasting God, who art always more ready to hear than we to pray, and art wont to give more than either we desire or deserve: Pour down upon us the abundance of thy mercy; forgiving us those things whereof our conscience is afraid, and giving us those good things which we are not worthy to ask, but through the merits and mediation of Jesus Christ, thy Son, our Lord. *Amen.*

The THIRTEENTH SUNDAY AFTER TRINITY

## THE THIRTEENTH SUNDAY AFTER TRINITY

ALMIGHTY and merciful God, of whose only gift it cometh that thy faithful people do unto thee true and laudable service: Grant, we beseech thee, that we may so faithfully serve thee in this life, that we fail not finally to attain thy heavenly promises; through the merits of Jesus Christ our Lord. *Amen.*

## THE FOURTEENTH SUNDAY AFTER TRINITY

ALMIGHTY and everlasting God, give unto us the increase of faith, hope and charity; and, that we may obtain that which thou dost promise, make us to love that which thou dost command; through Jesus Christ our Lord. *Amen.*

## THE FIFTEENTH SUNDAY AFTER TRINITY

KEEP, we beseech thee, O Lord, thy Church with, thy perpetual mercy; and, because the frailty of man without thee cannot but fall, keep us ever by thy help from all things hurtful, and lead us to all things profitable to our salvation; through Jesus Christ our Lord. *Amen.*

## THE SIXTEENTH SUNDAY AFTER TRINITY

O LORD, we beseech thee, let thy continual pity cleanse and defend thy Church; and, because it cannot continue in safety without thy succour, preserve it evermore by thy help and goodness; through Jesus Christ our Lord. *Amen.*

## THE SEVENTEENTH SUNDAY AFTER TRINITY

LORD, we pray thee that thy grace may always prevent and follow us, and make us continually to be given to all good works; through Jesus Christ our Lord. *Amen.*

### THE EIGHTEENTH SUNDAY AFTER TRINITY

LORD, we beseech thee, grant thy people grace to withstand the temptations of the world, the flesh and the devil, and with pure hearts and minds to follow thee the only God; through Jesus Christ our Lord. *Amen.*

### THE NINETEENTH SUNDAY AFTER TRINITY

O GOD, forasmuch as without thee we are not able to please thee; Mercifully grant, that thy Holy Spirit may in all things direct and rule our hearts; through Jesus Christ our Lord. *Amen.*

### THE TWENTIETH SUNDAY AFTER TRINITY

O ALMIGHTY and most merciful God, of thy bountiful goodness keep us, we beseech thee, from all things that may hurt us; that we, being ready both in body and soul, may cheerfully accomplish those things that thou wouldest have done; through Jesus Christ our Lord. *Amen.*

### THE TWENTY-FIRST SUNDAY AFTER TRINITY

GRANT, we beseech thee, merciful Lord, to thy faithful people pardon and peace; that they may be cleansed from all their sins, and serve thee with a quiet mind; through Jesus Christ our Lord. *Amen.*

### THE TWENTY-SECOND SUNDAY AFTER TRINITY

LORD, we beseech thee to keep thy household the Church in continual godliness; that through thy protection it may be free from all adversities, and devoutly given to serve thee in good works, to the glory of thy name; through Jesus Christ our Lord.

*Amen.*

### THE TWENTY-THIRD SUNDAY AFTER TRINITY

O GOD, our refuge and strength, who art the author of all godliness: Be ready, we beseech thee, to hear the devout prayers of thy Church; and grant that those things which we ask faithfully we may obtain effectually; through Jesus Christ our Lord.

*Amen.*

### THE TWENTY-FOURTH SUNDAY AFTER TRINITY

O LORD, we beseech thee, absolve thy people from their offences; that through thy bountiful goodness we may all be delivered from the bands of those sins, which by our frailty we have committed: Grant this, O heavenly Father, for Jesus Christ's sake, our blessed Lord and Saviour. *Amen.*

### THE SUNDAY NEXT BEFORE ADVENT

STIR up, we beseech thee, O Lord, the wills of thy faithful people; that they, plenteously bringing forth the fruit of good works, may of thee be plenteously rewarded; through Jesus Christ our Lord.

*Amen.*

## SAINT ANDREW'S DAY
### November 30

ALMIGHTY God, who didst give such grace unto the holy Apostle Saint Andrew, that he readily obeyed the calling of thy Son Jesus Christ, and followed him without delay: Grant unto us all, that we, being called by thy holy word, may forthwith give up ourselves obediently to fulfil thy holy commandments; through the same Jesus Christ our Lord. *Amen.*

## SAINT THOMAS THE APOSTLE
### December 21

ALMIGHTY and everliving God, who for the more confirmation of the faith didst suffer thy holy Apostle Thomas to be doubtful in thy Son's resurrection: Grant us so perfectly, and without all doubt, to believe in thy Son Jesus Christ, that our faith in thy sight may never be reproved. Hear us, O Lord, through the same Jesus Christ, to whom, with thee and the Holy Ghost, be all honour and glory, now and for evermore. *Amen.*

Saint Andrew

Saint Thomas

## THE CONVERSION OF SAINT PAUL
### January 25

O GOD, who, through the preaching of the blessed Apostle Saint Paul, hast caused the light of the Gospel to shine throughout the world: Grant, we beseech thee, that we, having his wonderful conversion in remembrance, may shew forth our thankfulness unto thee for the same, by following the holy doctrine which he taught; through Jesus Christ our Lord.                                   *Amen.*

## THE PRESENTATION OF CHRIST
## IN THE TEMPLE
### COMMONLY CALLED
## THE PURIFICATION OF
## SAINT MARY THE VIRGIN
### February 2

A LMIGHTY and everliving God, we humbly beseech thy Majesty, that, as thy only-begotten Son was this day presented in the temple in substance of our flesh, so we may be presented unto thee with pure and clean hearts, by the same thy Son Jesus Christ our Lord.                                   *Amen.*

The Conversion
of Saint Paul

The Purification of
Saint Mary the Virgin

The ANNUNCIATION of the BLESSED VIRGIN MARY

## SAINT MATTHIAS'S DAY
### February 24

O ALMIGHTY God, who into the place of the traitor Judas didst choose thy faithful servant Matthias to be of the number of the twelve Apostles: Grant that thy Church, being alway preserved from false Apostles, may be ordered and guided by faithful and true pastors; through Jesus Christ our Lord.

*Amen.*

## THE ANNUNCIATION OF THE BLESSED VIRGIN MARY
### March 25

WE beseech thee, O Lord, pour thy grace into our hearts; that, as we have known the incarnation of thy Son Jesus Christ by the message of an angel, so by his cross and passion we may be brought unto the glory of his resurrection; through the same Jesus Christ our Lord. *Amen.*

## SAINT MARK'S DAY
### April 25

O ALMIGHTY God, who hast instructed thy holy Church with the heavenly doctrine of thy Evangelist Saint Mark: Give us grace, that, being not like children carried away with every blast of vain doctrine, we may be established in the truth of thy holy Gospel; through Jesus Christ our Lord. *Amen.*

## SAINT PHILIP AND SAINT JAMES'S DAY
### May 1

O ALMIGHTY God, whom truly to know is ever lasting life: Grant us perfectly to know thy Son Jesus Christ to be the way, the truth, and the life; that, following the steps of thy holy Apostles, Saint Philip and Saint James, we may steadfastly walk in the way that leadeth to eternal life; through the same thy Son Jesus Christ our Lord. *Amen.*

## SAINT BARNABAS THE APOSTLE
### June 11

O LORD God Almighty, who didst endue thy holy Apostle Barnabas with singular gifts of the Holy Ghost: Leave us not, we beseech thee, destitute of thy manifold gifts, nor yet of grace to use them alway to thy honour and glory; through Jesus Christ our Lord. *Amen.*

Saint Philip & Saint James

Saint Barnabas the Apostle

## SAINT JOHN BAPTIST'S DAY
### June24

ALMIGHTY God, by whose providence thy servant John Baptist was wonderfully born, and sent
to prepare the way of thy Son our Saviour, by
preaching of repentance: Make us so to follow his
doctrine and holy life, that we may truly repent
according to his preaching, and after his example
constantly speak the truth, boldly rebuke vice, and
patiently suffer for the truth's sake; through Jesus
Christ our Lord.                                    *Amen.*

## SAINT PETER'S DAY
### June29

O ALMIGHTY God, who by thy Son Jesus Christ
didst give to thy Apostle Saint Peter many excellent gifts, and commandedst him earnestly to feed
thy flock: Make, we beseech thee, all Bishops and
Pastors diligently to preach thy holy Word, and the
people obediently to follow the same, that they may
receive the crown of everlasting glory; through Jesus
Christ our Lord.                                    *Amen.*

Saint John the
Baptist

Saint Peter

### SAINT JAMES THE APOSTLE
#### July 25

GRANT, O merciful God, that as thine holy Apostle Saint James, leaving his father and all that he had, without delay was obedient unto the calling of thy Son Jesus Christ, and followed him; so we, forsaking all worldly and carnal affections, may be evermore ready to follow thy holy commandments; through Jesus Christ our Lord.          *Amen.*

### SAINT BARTHOLOMEW THE APOSTLE
#### August 24

O ALMIGHTY and everlasting God, who didst give to thine Apostle Bartholomew grace truly to believe and to preach thy Word: Grant, we beseech thee, unto thy Church, to love that Word which he believed, and both to preach and receive the same; through Jesus Christ our Lord.          *Amen.*

### SAINT MATTHEW THE APOSTLE
#### September 21

O ALMIGHTY God, who by thy blessed Son didst call Matthew from the receipt of custom to be an Apostle and Evangelist: Grant us grace to forsake all covetous desires and inordinate love of riches, and to follow the same thy Son Jesus Christ, who liveth and reigneth with thee and the Holy Ghost, one God, world without end.          *Amen.*

## SAINT MICHAEL AND ALL ANGELS
### September 29

O EVERLASTING God, who hast ordained and constituted the services of Angels and men in a wonderful order: Mercifully grant that, as thy holy Angels alway do thee service in heaven, so by thy appointment they may succour and defend us on earth; through Jesus Christ our Lord.       *Amen.*

## SAINT LUKE THE EVANGELIST
### October 18

A LMIGHTY God, who calledst Luke the Physician, whose praise is in the Gospel, to be an Evangelist, and Physician of the soul: May it please thee that, by the wholesome medicines of the doctrine delivered by him, all the diseases of our souls may be healed; through the merits of thy Son Jesus Christ our Lord.       *Amen.*

Saint Luke the
✦ Evangelist ✦

## SAINT SIMON AND
## SAINT JUDE, APOSTLES
### October 28

O ALMIGHTY God, who hast built thy Church upon the foundation of the Apostles and Prophets, Jesus Christ himself being the head corner-stone: Grant us so to be joined together in unity of spirit by their doctrine, that we may be made an holy temple acceptable unto thee; through Jesus Christ our Lord. *Amen.*

## ALL SAINTS' DAY
### November 1

O ALMIGHTY God, who hast knit together thine elect in one communion and fellowship, in the mystical body of thy Son Christ our Lord: Grant us grace so to follow thy blessed Saints in all virtuous and godly living, that we may come to those unspeakable joys, which thou hast prepared for them that unfeignedly love thee; through Jesus Christ our Lord. *Amen.*

S. Simon & S. Jude

All Saints Day

## COLLECTS FROM THE
## ORDER OF THE HOLY COMMUNION

ALMIGHTY God, unto whom all hearts be open, all desires known, and from whom no secrets are hid: Cleanse the thoughts of our hearts by the inspiration of thy Holy Spirit, that we may perfectly love thee, and worthily magnify thy holy Name; through Christ our Lord. *Amen.*

ASSIST us mercifully, O Lord, in these our supplications and prayers, and dispose the way of thy servants towards the attainment of everlasting salvation; that, among all the changes and chances of this mortal life, they may ever be defended by thy most gracious and ready help; through Jesus Christ our Lord. *Amen.*

ALMIGHTY Lord, and everlasting God, vouchsafe, we beseech thee, to direct, sanctify and govern, both our hearts and bodies, in the ways of thy laws, and in the works of thy commandments; that through thy most mighty protection, both here and ever, we may be preserved in body and soul; through our Lord and Saviour Jesus Christ. *Amen.*

GRANT, we beseech thee, Almighty God, that the words, which we have heard this day with our outward ears, may through thy grace be so grafted inwardly in our hearts, that they may bring forth in us the fruit of good living, to the honour and praise of thy Name; through Jesus Christ our Lord. *Amen.*

PREVENT US, O Lord, in all our doings with thy most gracious favour, and further us with thy continual help; that in all our works, begun, continued, and ended in thee, we may glorify thy holy Name, and finally by thy mercy obtain everlasting life; through Jesus Christ our Lord. *Amen.*

ALMIGHTY God, the fountain of all wisdom, who knowest our necessities before we ask, and our ignorance in asking: We beseech thee to have compassion upon our infirmities; and those things, which for our unworthiness we dare not, and for our blindness we cannot ask, vouchsafe to give us for the worthiness of thy Son Jesus Christ our Lord. *Amen.*

ALMIGHTY God, who hast promised to hear the petitions of them that ask in thy Son's Name: We beseech thee mercifully to incline thine ears to us that have made now our prayers and supplications unto thee; and grant that those things, which we have faithfully asked according to thy will, may effectually be obtained, to the relief of our necessity, and to the setting forth of thy glory; through Jesus Christ our Lord. *Amen.*

# AFTERWORD BY THE BISHOP OF LONDON

The Collects assembled in the Book of Common *Prayer* offer departure at all gates into the mystery of the God "whose ways are not our ways and whose thoughts are not our thoughts". Here is no godlet confected out of our own fantasies; no neighbourhood god jogging with us through life's way but here is the entry into the God "whom no man hath seen at any time", who has been made known by "the only begotten Son which is in the bosom of the Father".

The spirit of these ancient prayers has little of the improper confidence of those who are pally with Sion. By contrast these prayers approach the divine mystery by way of a defamiliarizing ceremoniousness and a shocking reverence which for those with ears to hear can deliver us from the waking dream in which humanity and not God is the centre around which the whole universe revolves. We have begun to appreciate the cost of believing that we are licensed to exploit, without limit, all that exists. These are prayers for use in a day when it is vital once again to respect the distance between God and human beings. Such respect is an indispensable preparation for wisdom and for any profound appreciation of the work of Jesus Christ in reconciling us to God.

Those who have the privilege of leading the worship of the Church in these words will always know themselves as "the ministers and stewards of thy mysteries and not as the managers of some Spirit Shop catering for popular religious tastes and feelings. I hope and pray that this volume will introduce a new generation to this treasury of prayer and I commend the zeal and efforts of the Prayer Book Society in ensuring that, like Richard Hooker in a similar time of crisis, "Posterity may know that we have not loosely through silence permitted things to pass away as in a dream".

"Almighty and everlasting God, who art always more ready to hear than we to pray, and art wont to give more than either we desire, or deserve: Pour down upon us the abundance of thy mercy; forgiving those things whereof our conscience is afraid, and giving us those good things which we are not worthy to ask, but through the merits and mediation of Jesus Christ, thy Son, our Lord. Amen"

*Richard London:*